ACKNOWLEDGMNT

A Book of this nature could not have been written in isolation.

Therefore I would like to acknowledge the assistance received from some people, some blogs and some corporate bodies in the course of the work.

To everyone, blog and every corporate body that in one way or the other helps in the production of this book. I want to say a big Thank You to you all.

DEDICATION

This book is dedicated to everyone that is willing to make a passive income online and anyone that finds it easier to work from home.

It is dedicated to You.

INTRODUCTION

Making money online have been a way many people have indeed really sought for but many doesn't know how to go about it, this book provides a quick guide to make passive income online that can be digested within some minutes and get started with the referenced sites and blogs highlighted in the book.

TABLE OF CONTENT

- **CHAPTER ONE**
  THE TRUTH ABOUT MAKING MONEY ONLINE.

- **CHAPTER TWO**
  DIFFERENT WAYS TO MAKE PASSIVE INCOME ONLINE AND FROM HOME.

MAKE MONEY ONLINE (QUICK GUIDE)

CHAPTER ONE

THE TRUTH ABOUT MAKING MONEY ONLINE

For some people, making money online pleases them than working in companies and under someone that governs their time and denied them of their selves. If this people could find a way to make money working at home or online, they would be very happy and can even vacate the current work they are doing and focus more on making money online which will allow them to spend more time with their families and loved ones, and they would be in charge of their time without anyone governing or controlling them and their time.

The fact about this is that; earning money online isn't a folk tales or story, it is real and possible, over the times many people believes it is not a genuine means of making money while some taught it is not an easier way to make money. I have been making money online for a while now and I'm a living testimony to confirm you can make money online. I also know many a person who are making money online or from home in different ways, and that is because there are several and varieties of ways to make money online depending on the aspects you are best at. Some take courses, some market strategies and so on.

Now, here's the good news. Most of the online money making platform are not that complicated, you just have to take time and read and understand how each platform works, and once you get it, you will be amazed to see things changing around. Like any business venture, your online income takes time to grow. You devote the time and energy required to get your idea off the ground, and you need focus and determination when it seems it getting slow to get off the ground because you just started.

If you're willing to make money online but aren't sure where to start, here are several and well selected platform to start.

CHAPTER TWO

DIFFERENT WAYS TO MAKE PASSIVE INCOME ONLINE AND FROM HOME

- **Make money through Google Ad sense**

Have you visited any site before and you saw Google ads. These ads are everywhere, and for good reason. They are not only easy to setup but also profitable as far as your website starts bringing in a steady amount of traffic or as far as many people do visit your website or blog.

You can have a blog or website created for you if you do not have one, because this ads sense will favor someone that has blog or website and has what it takes to attracts traffic or people which means that your website or blog must be equipped with suiting and interesting contents.

One of the amazing things about Google Ads Sense is that it's very easy to get set up. If you have a blog or website, you can sign up for a free Google Ads Sense Account. Google will then give you a unique code which you will paste on your website or blog. Google takes it from there, they track your traffic, page, earning and get you your shares. The sweet thing is that you do not need to stress yourself, they will do the most for you, and yours is just to set it up and it's not a hard one.

How much can I make with Google ads sensor? You can make as much as you can, this depends on time and your blog and website traffic, a friend of mine earn nothing less than $4,500 per month from his website. Thou it wasn't like that when he started, but as time goes by and pass by it started yielding well. That was why I mentioned being focus and determined earlier.

- **Consulting**

Another easiest way to make money online and work from home is through consulting. If you're an expert in any field, you could reach out to people out there and help them with their problems regarding your field using your experience to solve different difficulties of the people and they pay you for your service as long as it is helpful and good enough to solve their problem. You can also render services to big companies and help them with a particular problem, yes you can! Don't look down on yourself and because you might end up bewildered as to how much they offer to pay for the services.

A friend of mine Daniel Ryan told me that he was into blogging for some years ago and many people knew him with the blog and he is never relenting thou it first seems to be non encouraging, but later over the years, he was very vast with the operation and marketing strategy, only to see a mail from a company on one faithful day, he opened the mail and first taught it was a joke, but it wasn't, the company wanted him to get them through some marketing strategy, at a point, he charges $80 per hour and the session was about how to use face book and some other social media platform to grow their brand.

If now you want to start consulting but you are not sure of where to start, you can set up a free account via **clarity.fm** this website lets those who want to offer consulting set up a free profile and let them be reachable to the people. Once your profile is set up, people will start finding you and book a session you'll get paid for.

- **Offer online Courses**

Do you have a skill you can teach others, if yes! It is possible you set up an online course. By setting up an online course, you could make lucrative amount by teaching people what you know how to do and what you find easier to do.

Many people set up their courses online via platform like **Teachable.com**. With this website, you can upload the materials of the courses you wanted to take and use the platform to manage customers and accept payments with ease.

Some other online resources for teaching courses includes: **Teach.udemy.com**, **Takelesson.com, Skillshare.com**, you could upload books in PDF format, word format, downloadable slides and so on, and you can also do live videos to reach the heart of your students.

- **Book Sales and publishing**

This might first look somehow to you, but the good news is; thou the publishing companies are known for heavy tasks, but nowadays, you can complete the uploading, publishing, printing and marketing all online with ease. Websites like **createspace.com or Kdp.amazon.com** will let you upload your book and take your book to print and even get it delivered for you without getting a formal publisher involved. This website will make your book visible on the book stores and online market space.

If you think you are capable enough to write a book people would love to buy, this is an easy way to get it done and make your money since the start-up costs can be very minimal and you probably already have a computer gadget and word processing software to get things done for you. But if you are going into this, please make sure your books are well written and edited to attract customers and sales.

- **Become a Freelancer**

If you have the skill to write and do creative things, you can make money and get paid online becoming a freelancer. This very one needs your focus and determination as well, and you have to be loyal and deliver quality work on time so as to attract more customers and more reviews as well as more recommendations.

According to John, the success key to making it as a freelance writer is getting and figuring out a niche you are expert at, then networking with people who might hire you or needs your services and delivering high quality work on time. Thou there are several freelance websites, but as to John experience, he said it is easier to start up with websites like **Upwork.com.**

- **Make money through Sponsored Posts**

If you own a website or you have many social media followers, you can also make money by pursuing sponsored posts and ads. But how does this work? Basically, big companies are willing to pay bloggers and social media influencers to promote their products and services. If you have a platform that many people flow on, be it a blog or a many Instagram followers, you can surely make good use of all these you have to make some money.

The first time I got a sponsored post for Good Financial Cents, it was amazing. But then it was a little cent around $150. As time goes by, however, I realized organizations that wanted a sponsored post really just wanted a link from my website to their own site. For that, I started adding up to the rate I charge.

Nowadays I charge $4,000 cent and above for a sponsored post.

I also know some bloggers that get $30,000 for a sponsored post. That's cool right? That's to show how much you can make through sponsored post. Actually, you don't need to have a website to do sponsored content since you can get it done and get paid if you have a lot of social media followers.

- **Make money through Webinars**

Another idea on how to make money online and from home is using webinars to market your product, service, or course. I've done webinars to promote my financial planning practice and to boom up interest in my online course for financial advisors and students. With webinar, you're actually offering a lot of tips, hints and advice for free — mostly in a live format. And at the end though, you pitch your paid product or service with the aim of securing some deals.

Professional speakers use webinars to market their courses on public speaking and speech delivery.

Regardless of what you're selling, it's not really that hard to set up a webinar and attract people to sign up with a lead magnet or Facebook ads. Nevertheless, you can probably find a free webinar on how and ways to create your first webinar if you look hard enough online and enough that worth it.

- **YouTube**

YouTube is another cool and money making platform that has really made it easy and possible for people to earn money online. There are a millions of YouTube channels out there on any topic you can think of, and most people with a many followers are earning cool money in exchange for their videos and time took to make the videos.

Regardless of your current field, you can actually make YouTube a sideway of making cool cash, I know of a civil engineer that upload videos about Men's wear and he is really hitting it. If you know any other thing including topics relating to your field, you can make money creating a video about cool topics and make cool money!

How to videos are also best starts on YouTube.

- **Tutor**

Another easy way to take advantage of your skills online is: Become an online tutor. The website **cambly.com** helps you get paid to chat with people from around the whole world. As the tutorial is ongoing, the site will automatically tracks the time you spent online, paying close to or exactly $10.20 an hour. Thou that might sounds like a small cent, consider the fact that you can actually set your own hours, work as little or as much as you want—and if you're living in some certain location , $10.20 an hour can go a long way indeed.

- **Become a Juror**

This favors mostly those that in the line of law. Here's a case where you won't dread jury duty.

The site **eJury.com** has indeed revolutionized the way lawyers prepare for trial by creating on-net or online mock juries and focus groups that help attorneys determine prepare case. You'll get paid for participating.

- **Become a Virtual Assistant**

Are you indeed organized and resourceful? As a virtual assistant, you make money online by helping people companies, businesses with tasks ranging from data entry to research to customer service.

Vanenetworking.com was founded by a virtual assistant and is equipped with tips and job leads that will get you cool money.

- **Teach English**

Many taught you need to be living abroad in order to teach English to foreigners or foreign students. But as GoOverseas.com points out, "With video chatting and conferencing growing easier and more reliable every year, teaching English lessons online is another great way to fund your life abroad or at home." Rates for teaching English language online can go for up to $20 per hour.

- **Make money online by selling your photos and videos online**

Are you a photo lover? Or you like taking beautiful pictures of nature, houses, animals, people and many other beautiful things? Photography and video making can be a good way to earn money online. Stock websites make it easy for photographers and videographers to upload their work, and then they will market on your behalf and create income for you while you were off shooting the next beautiful location and photos. Stock agencies looking for submissions include:

submit.shutterstock.com,

Photoshelter.com,

Fotolia.com and

istockphoto.com.

- **Make money online by creating software reviews**

Do you have strong opinions on software? either positive or negative opinion, you can get paid for creating reviews online. **Softwarejudge.com** is a good place to take a start.

- **Getting Crafty**

Are you a crafty entrepreneur? You can actually earn money online through what you do. Many people know the popular site **Etsy.com**, which is a online marketplace for handmade items. But recently you can actually sell your jewelry and other handmade wares on sites like: services.amazon.com/handmade/handmade.html

services.amazon.com/handmade/handmade.html,

Artfire.com,

Cargoh.com and more.

- **Set up a Content and Web Development Business**

Are you an expert in creating web and content development? You can offer these services to anyone and companies through online tools that make developing beautiful websites a snap. Some resources to get this done include:

Wordpress.com,

Weebly.com and

Joomla.org.

- **Type and transcribe for Cash**

Are you fast at typing? Transcribing is simple: You listen to an audio file through headphones and type it out. Mostly as a transcriber you get paid as fast as you can type. "Transcription jobs are paid by the audio hour (the length of the audio file), rather than by the hour worked. The time spent on a transcript is sometimes influenced and determined by the quality of the audio, the background noise, the accent of the speaker and the speed at which people speaks." You can take a look at the company **rev.com/freelancers**, which hires freelance transcribers.

- **Create a Money-Making Blog**

Do you have an area you are expert in? Share your advice on a blog site. And if travelling is your area of expertise, you can think about what you have to offer the people or companies.

You can actually create a blog to upload advices, tips and guide relating to what you are expert in or what is related to your filed of work. The more traffic that patronize your site, the more you earn. The sites:

Squarespace.com/tour/create-a-blog/ and

Wix.com/start/blog have tips on how to create blogs and can also host them.

The Bottom Line

There are a ridiculous many number of ways to make money online and the ones I've covered here are just an inch in foots. If you have time, a passion for almost anything, and at least some creative skill, you may be able to build an online income stream — or several — if you give it enough time.

But, don't just take my word as it said. If you search online, you'll find thousands of success stories you can use for inspiration and motivations.

One day you could even create a success story of your own. But you'll never know unless you try.

THANKS FOR READING…

(IF YOU FOUND THIS BOOK INTERESTING, PLEASE CONSIDER LEAVING AN HONEST REPLY ON YOUR FAVOURITE STORE)

For more books to keep company with friends and families: check out the following books by the same author (ROB MORRIS)

1) The best joke book ever! (For all ages) book 1 (series book {the giggle book}) by Rob Morris.

2) The best joke book ever! (For all ages) books 2 by Rob Morris.

3) Tricky riddles and brain teaser book for kids and teens by Rob Morris.

4) How to fix and get past a broken heart by John Morris.

5) Funniest joke book (for all ages) by Rob Morris.

Search for all on amazon.com and be surprised as to the message they all have to pass.

www.ingramcontent.com/pod-product-compliance
Lightning Source LLC
Chambersburg PA
CBHW050324220526
45465CB00005B/2114